Love, Lust, & Life

By

Ron Whitaker, Jr.

COLLEGE BOY
PUBLISHING
"We Breed Bestsellers"

POETRY/INSPIRATIONAL/MEMOIR

ISBN: 978-1-944110-46-8

Edited by **Armani Valentino**

for College Boy Publishing. LLC

Published for print & digital distribution by **Armani Valentino**
Inside Designed & Setup by **Armani Valentino**

Cover Design by Armani Valentino for College Boy Publishing
Pre-Edits by Tia Day for College Boy Publishing, LLC

Published in Dallas, TX, by College Boy Publishing. College Boy Publishing is a division of The College Boy Company & ArmaniValentino.com. Wholesale copies of this book may be ordered directly from the publisher at www.collegeboypublishing.com. Please allow up to 7-10 Business Days for delivery.. Call 972-383-9234

Ron Whitaker, Jr. aka VaKation is available for professional counseling sessions, workshops, panel discussions, consultations, and radio & television interviews contact 972-781-8404.

Printed in the United States of America

08 09 10 11 12 RWJAV 5 4 3 2 1

Love, Lust, & Life

Written By

Ron Whitaker, Jr.

Dedication

I would like to dedicate this book to every woman I've ever came in contact with whether it be as a lover, close friends or indirectly in passing I thank God for you. I appreciate you for just being whom you are.

I admired your strength and your nurturing spirit and your ability to make the darkest days seems as if they are the brightest ones. You have been entrusted with such a precious gift the ability to bring forth life you are unique, you are loved and you are appreciated.

Love—Pg. 1

Lust—Pg. 33

Life—Pg. 51

Love, Lust, & Life

Love

Literally, Mentally, Lyrically, Physically

June 13, 2011 at 8:40pm

Literally you lure me lyrically with your lips
Kisses so soft followed by a warm embrace
It's me expressing my gratitude for the
Ability to view your smile on a daily basis...

I wouldn't trade the thought of you
For the treasure she possesses in her physical

Mentally you captivate my attention
And send subliminal messages to my peak
In its peak, so even when I'm asleep
Your persona takes precedence over my thoughts,
in dreams and visions....
So I envision you when I'm awake and
Talk to you until I fall asleep...

2

May 2, 2011 at 7:48pm

The love that I have for you
Surpasses all words and expressions that I have ever felt..
You're my lifeline
I feel you in my bloodline...
My genes are filled with you
My physical and mental both come from you...
I am an expression of the two of you...
With you sometimes I don't know what to do...
So I just love and pray for you...
Sometimes from a distance,
But it goes without mention that I am you.

The better of two halves spilt equally into the perfect whole...
So I feel you even when you're distant...
Because your thoughts and actions are familiar to me
When I see you I see me, in the literal sense…
Even if I'm observing you in the present tense
My future reference is where we started....
From a long list of thoughts in the heat of several moments
We were physically formed in love...
Mi familia...

Mi Amor

April 1, 2011 at 1:56am

Mi amor, I refuse to let you go
Seeing that the absence of your presence is still present
in your absence....
So presently I'm present-less...
In desperate need of my better half
Seeing that I'm only a portion of what I was.... It's obvi-
ous your synopsis is a part of me...
So hurting you is like killing me...
Since we're one body, what's yours is mine and what's
mine is yours
Even my whole body...
I'm immune to everyone and I don't want anybody but
you...
She's the air I breathe
She's the closest thing to me besides me
She's my oxygen...
But now she's the only antigen
I can detect her in my immediate vicinity
Enabling my ability to be who I should be
The woman of my dreams
A.K.A... Ms. Who is she???

Connection

February 28, 2011 at 1:02pm

How can I live if I can't breathe...?
How am I expected to rest if I can't sleep?
And all my energy is gone because I can't eat...

Tossing and turning between sheets
Can't find sleep...
And she's heavy on my mind but
Our connection is weak...

I tried to contact her but
Every other word is a bleep...
Signal fade, call lost...
Now I'm lost!
Surrounded by darkness and uncertain thoughts...

Looking for something that seems familiar to me...
But the more I think about it,
I realize this is all new to me...
"Unfamiliar territory..."
So let our thoughts and actions tell the story
Not for what it was
But for what it could be...
Assuming nothing but the reality

Addiction

December 12, 2010 at 11:29pm

Abase in the abyss of its admission...
Intervention came to mind, but they're on the
outside looking in...
This drug's addiction is strong and I'm feeling
weak
Fuck it!!!
I'd rather suffer the addiction and deal with the
consequences later...
This one thing I can't do without...
No matter what they said or
What y'all say...
It doesn't matter!!!... I'm trapped
Now I'm giving in to this one thing willfully
Accepting the side effects of its hold,
Whether their up, down or everywhere
I'm too far in now!
If it's not the death of me, it's definitely
On the battlefield worth fighting for...
This addiction is me
This addiction is we
This addiction is us
Honestly...This addiction is she

Your Time
March 13, 2013

All I need is your mind, attention, and a little of your time

To make sure your mind is at ease...

Give me your trust
If that's not asking too much

I know loyalty and faithfulness are rare commodities...

But it doesn't take astrology to explain the chemistry we possess

Although the situation is different the solution is the same...

All I need is your mind, attention, and a bit of your time

Love

February 21, 2013 at 8:09am

From the start I've loved you
You've given me a reason to trust
Through all of our obstacles
you never left me without love....
So I could never leave you
You have my heart
And you showed me how to lower my guard
God knows my soul mate was sent
When you arrived in my life
My lover... My friend...
My life...

Mesmerized

February 14, 2013 at 10:25am

The sun danced across her face,
And then the rain stopped....
For a moment everything revolved around her
Or at least I did...
She had my son
She was my queen and I was her king
I would move the moon to give her stars
Clustered in diamonds, and…
Stop time just to rewind it
Rethink it just to remind her
Leave notes as a reminder
That her best days are still ahead
And her past is all behind her

Unfamiliar Feeling

November 5, 2012 at 9:19pm

Unfamiliar feeling baby because I'm a rebel
I'm on my way to go get her
I think we're better together
I pray her prayers have been answered and
I'm exactly what she needs
I'm serious about her like a 1000 decrees,
7 continents, I'll swim across the 7 seas
No make believe
Just to put her at ease
The masculine producer of her seed
Should've been me
I put it all on the line
Addressed to her so she knew it was me
If you understand this enigma you're better than me
I only understand what I write
When I say it in threes (3's)

The Message

November 4, 2012 at 5:30pm

What's understood ain't got to be said,
So, we said nothing...
And continued having a mental discussion
With our eyes in public...
Enjoying the moment
Life is full of options,
But I'm interested in her rushes
I'm feeling you so much,
But we aren't even touching
I don't completely understand the connection
But in order for the lights to come on,
Something has got to be electric
And to pass a test, you first have to be tested...
I'm in love with her eyes, smile, and her essence
Just lying here with her, in some instances,
Is better than sex is...
I said it because I meant it
I hope she got the message

Subconscious Manifest

June 7, 2012 at 9:21pm

Some say the preservation of relations
Are no longer relevant in this present tense
But the Mark that you made was permanent
And to think
We almost never met....
A letter without an address,
But it read *Heaven Sent...*
I sent you a gift, and
If you keep and treat it as such
I'd let you have it
And you could teach it to the masses

Strangers

April 17, 2012 at 10:33am

Met a perfect stranger and it was stranger that she
knew me...
Said she heard me at the spot when I was displaying
my art
She was in attendance with the audience and at-
tempted to get my attention
She said she loved the way I recite lines and to take this
It was her number between two lines
And a small note attached that said,
"Read between lines and let's just live this life away
from lies...
Starting from this one vibe...
I promise I would never leave your side..."
And I replied, "It sounds good and beautiful, but I
have a wife and to her I would never lie."
However, I lied because didn't have a wife
But I had a reason for leaving
Let's just call it a "business meeting..."
With a beautiful woman
I met the other evening
And you're just a stranger

My Inspiration

January 24, 2012 at 10:03am

I found inspiration in her eyes as I've done so many
times
But this time she knows exactly where my
inspiration lies...
In search of the truth once distracted by lies,
In Life patience is a virtue
And in certain aspects, that's how I run mine
I would rather live alone than without her in my life
One life to live
So I think twice about my wrongs and
acknowledge all my rights
Because I would rather have patience than to ever live
a lie in this life

Traces of You

January 17, 2012 at 5:38pm

The residue from your first impression is still fairly new
Although I've heard from you, the blessing was my
pleasure in meeting you,
You're spiritual and visual
There's no comparing you
You're all alone in a zone
You're what I compare them to
Day and night at the slightest and certain variables,
They can't be you
So they try terribly to bury you,
Under obstacles and scenarios
Exposing themselves open like 24s...
Corner stores in the hood
Where the doors never close
Her mind is open...
She's blunt, but she keeps her legs closed...
Until her feelings are peaked
And are kicking in doors...
A rush to get her out of her clothes
And take my time behind these closed doors

To You

December 14, 2011 at 12:47pm

I admired you from a distance
Indirectly composing lines about you
That would appeal to the ears of the masses
But to decipher these thoughts
You would need 3D glasses
Shot glasses and an astray to dump these ashes
Because to me you embody perfection in one body
And physically your body stimulates my senses and
Sends me senseless into a catastrophic world wind
And I pretend every potential hook up is with you
I don't even see them
All I see is you
Part of me is saying all I need is you
But in the meantime, in between time
I'll just release these words into existence
Hoping that they would find their way to you
And back to me
The irony of mental intimacy
Written down but never spoken verbally
To You...

With Tears in Her Eyes

July 9, 2014 at 6:29am

I looked deeply into her eyes
And teleported her thoughts into mine
Made love to her mind
Minus the physical contact and turned up her vibe
I told her the truth and
Filtered out all the lies
And spoke on life as if it was just her and I ...
Mended to together two veils to align
Coexisting through the thick & thin of the hardest time
"I even got your back baby when you're too weak to have mine."
But I do realize with every emotion that you hold inside
That we would do it all over again
Just to say that we tried

Absent Love

July 15, 2014 at 3:56am

In the back of her mind she sometimes wonders
If she had ever met him before
Had their paths ever crossed, or...
Was he just a thought created by her own imagination?

Someone who would love her like the bones of his own flesh, and...
Protect her like the heart from his chest
Trust and communicate about her insecurities
Until none are left

Massage her body and kiss her lips
Breathe life into her dreams
Motivate her to be better than she even thought possible
Love and loyalty defeats every obstacle
In her mind the absence of the two wouldn't at all be logical

Nonverbal Communication

April 18, 2014 at 7:25am

I looked into her eyes and heard her heart speak.

It said…

"I don't need your security,
But I want to feel secure in your circumference.

I want to hide my insecurities in your conscience,
And be consumed by your love and trust in me.

The irony of our reality sounds like make believe.

But if you believe in love,
Believe in me."

Homie Lover Friend

January 9, 2014 at 2:39pm

It started out as a game
We entertained each other with lies...
Now it doesn't feel the same
Unless you're lying by my side...

Never mind what the naysayers says
Let the haters hate
They're just jealous babe...

What we have can't be duplicated
And in its physical form it feels amazing
We share a bond like we're related
Down for each other like the pavement
And I'm complacent when were together
Just pacing...

Soul Mate

November 30, 2013 at 6:11pm

What if I told you I was a thief
And my only intention was to steal your heart
And make it mine...
Spend time, share my life;
Learn the ins and outs of your emotions
So that I would never make you cry
Only make you smile...

You are my light
As the light in my life I take you as you are
My friend, my lover, my wife
Anything that concerns you now concerns me
Complete honesty, faithfulness, and loyalty
Is my promise and my priority... to You!

Understand?

July 31, 2013 at 12:28pm

She used to love me for me
Now she loves me because she
Can call me when she's in need
I satisfy her needs
And to her difficulties I bring ease

Believe me when I say
I don't understand the transition,
But when we do what it is we do
We do it with precision

It transcends our understanding
Instantaneously making our connection understood
Do you understand?

Goodbye

June 18, 2013 at 4:57am

Trying to find time in the present
I lost sight of her smile and forgot to make her laugh
Couldn't be mad when she fell in the arms of another
You do the math…

I tried to love her
But my words couldn't explain my actions
Not enough similes, verbs, or metaphors
Could explain…
The absence of my presence

I'm acting on pure instinct
Intoxicated by Life's situations
Time steady turning
I'm trying to turn the tables
With intentions of moving commas
We reap what we sow; karma

Take my heart when you leave...

Us

May 9, 2013 at 7:17pm

Darkness fills the situation
Since we don't share emotions
Going through the motions
Isn't worth the effort....

Whether we weather the storm with our efforts
Is still a hidden endeavor
We want the best for each other
Even if that meant we would never stay together
We would have what we had and treasured that treasure

Together

April 26, 2013 at 10:06am

Painted a picture with her in mind
And sent it from a distance
Attachment with a sentence

My heart won't
Let me lose her
But I never chose to love her...
Wasting time before I met her
Now I don't want to let her go
I can't completely tell her in words, symbols, or letters
how I felt her

What started from one late night conversation
Has led us to recycling daylight
In the moonlight with flashlights
Glancing at timelines as time flies... TOGETHER

Naked Truth

See babe I could tell you lies that blend in between lines,
but...
To me that would be defeating the purpose
See...
Words without truth make the thought process null;
worthless...
Empty expressions serve no purpose...
Would it be different if you could ask me anything, and
know...
That I was telling you the truth about everything
Without hesitation...
Just another process of our progress
Truth be told babe I admire your physical,
But it's your mental that I'm really into
Even when I'm in you
And can feel your emotions running down
Like a waterfall within you
The naked truth is the server of the menu

Square Root of 2

Smooth conscience, calm, cool confidence
Confident collective countenance
Stone cold silhouette
Shadows fading in the distance
Smoke detectors defective because of the essence
We know who we are
No pretending, or fictional characters.
That's friction, physics, square roots, and methods
Scientific solutions…
Still chemistry
1.41421356237……
Irrational digits
Dig it and keep it

Time

Time is of the essence
No need for stressin'
Over nonsense
To taste, touch or feel you baby
That's beyond sense and all of our senses
No approval needed from the census
Because the negativity they begin now,
Baby that's senseless
When I don't see you
I'd rather think on how much I miss you
Then show you what the best do
Not only when I undress you
Or even when I sex you, but...
Stimulating conversation eliminate the stress too

Satisfied

April 13, 2010 at 10:34pm

The mere thought of you leaves me mesmerized,
Hypnotized in a sea of replies and sighs...
Oohs and Aahs
Even with my photographic memory
It's impossible for me to materialize
Or even emphasize
Why I visualize
Long days and nights spent between your thighs
Baby please realize
These are not white lies,
But words from the heart immortalized
Never been big on fantasies, but...
You make me fantasize
I feel light in the wind like butterflies
And I don't know the reason why
But somehow I'm satisfied

Emotions

April 2, 2010 at 1:36am

Baby...
All those emotions you try to hide,
I try to find before we crossed this line
You were a friend of mine
Now systematically in a rhyme,
We are intertwined horizontally in a line
And the experience is unlike I've ever had
No feeling bad... or feeling sad... or being mad...
But more like a breath of fresh air
You could go anywhere,
But in your mind, body, and soul... I'm present there
Long or short hair
Baby I don't care
And I was so desperately in need of this change
Now no need for change
I got my dime

Amazing

March 18, 2010 at 7:54pm

Some days I'm amazed
At the many ways you make me smile
All the while unaware of your actions concerning me
You're really learning me, or should I say learning we
WE ARE two pronouns attached by an apostrophe
Like French we agree, Oui Oui!
So why wouldn't we
Align our lives in a line attached at the Mind
Leaving pessimism behind
Only living and dying in us

Lust

Deeply Within Her

July 11, 2011 at 10:41pm

She's beautiful, strong and independent....
Her true character is tucked deeply within her secrets
So I navigate with a firm grip and a gentle kiss...
Ripping the seam of her dress...
Marking the spot with X's and O's
No words uttered, so all there is are X's and O's
New memories blended with old...

We're compatible, so what y'all say doesn't mean shit!!
She revealed to me her Victoria's,
And leaked her secrets...
No lights, we could barely see shit...
But with precision and my mental vision
I was able to make the key fit...

Fitting every groove
When she moves I'm induced by her movement...
She grips and pulls....
She scratches and bites...
I bury my jewels in the base of her secret place
Capacity full...
No open space...
Deeply within her

"Deeply Within Her " (Part 2)

July 13, 2011 at 1:48am

There is no open space......
Pleasure and pain is written all over your face
We switched positions and changed to a faster pace
The sound of drums beating
With my hands clinching your waist

Right, then left to a depth you've never had...
In and out
Temporary only when necessary
I'm back at it...
Systematic...
She's sensitive
With every touch she's spasmodic

Her body is crawling backwards, and...
Her walls are closing in
Her grip is tightening
Her body is stiffening up
I'm deeply within her
The treasure...
She gave it up

Mentally

April 13, 2011 at 5:28am

I concur with the idea of a mental conversation..
No words if that's what you're into...
Cursing in motion...
Ecstasy…
No pills...
Just overdosed mentally
Physically tired in the worst way
But it's a great thing!!!
All your senses within...
Running down your thoughts...
Ultimately making your body shake
Contracting your diaphragm...
You take in a breath so you don't suffocate
You understood me first
I over stood you last
Getting to the point of interest repeatedly...
Reviewing every detail
Do tell...
And explain why you chose that position
And view from that aspect.
And...
It's possible...
That your mental hasn't gained access
Or….
Experienced the assets…
Of profound knowledge over a smooth beat....
Mentally!

Lust of Love

January 12, 2011 at 1:13am

See the Lust of Love is an acquired taste
Served with a side of erotic etiquette...
Independent, strong, and delicate...

From inside to her silhouette
Images of her in my mind at night make my body sweat
Waking up next to her now has my body wet
Anticipating the best sex she could ever get

I can see it in her eyes
I'm stimulating her senses
To the point that we're senseless
Lost in a pool of us...
Living beyond existence...

Pleasure & Pain

Running out of our pores like sweat
We found ecstasy in the form of our essence
Entangled in a web of pleasure and pain...
It may hurt at first
But it's the pleasure of pain
Consistent with this new found addiction
Mixing and blending as she reached her climax mentally
Then her body exploded...
Systematically sending erosions to all her senses

Satisfaction

February 21, 2013

She's addicted to brown skin like sugar
Biting, kissing, licking, and wishing she could taste it
even when I'm gone...
Her sweet tooth is craving sweetness in my absence
Her thoughts are transparent and my actions are
always accurate
I do more than aim to please...
She came before me
And won't leave until she knows I am pleased...

I Paint It

April 30, 2012 at 9:35pm

I paint a perfect picture on her body so clear and vivid...
That when she's alone,
She closes her eyes to replay it until I revisit
Then we relived it...
Recorded it on camera phone...
I send it to her in a message and got a reply back...
"It's yours isn't it?"
I responded, "Yes," But you can keep it
As long as you keep it clean
And a secret, and
Anyone that seeks it when I'm gone
You would leave them delinquent

Honestly, I could be jealous of your fingers
When they're anywhere near it
When I'm anywhere near it, I'm in It

Making messes we don't mention
Without metaphors of similes
We paint away the tension
Create more vivid images
We paint... You paint it... I paint it!

I Paint....It (part 2)

May 2, 2012 at 11:39am

Completely saturated in sweaty sex
I'm certain we came at the same time
In the meantime in between time,
I'm in between, lying...
Laying it down trying to lay you out
I feel your legs vibrating and shaking
And the moves I'm making
In, out, right then left as I...
Pull your hair and smack your rear
You can image how soaked we are
Emotions floating everywhere...
As I said before, "I even envy your fingers…"
Because I'm that into you and systematically in rhyme
I want to get into you
Rip your clothes off to the bare minimum and swim in
your birthday suit….
Wrap you up...
And I won't stop until you reach the climax too
Interlude...
Then lift you up and re-enter you like an inner tube
I'm really into you
Started from the top
Replay, rewind, and continue until you quiver
And shiver too...

The Aim

October 4, 2011 at 8:28am

I'm accurate in aiming toward awesome and amazing
Hormones raging body language in Cajun
Patient in her purpose,
But she's overwhelmed by persuasion
And the mind blowing idea that led to this altercation
Experience the penetration
Both physically and mentally blazing
I can see that she's ready
I was anxiously waiting,
But she gave the invitation
Which gave me the confirmation
She signed the affidavit and told me I was her greatest
She arrived first
Just so excited that I made it...
Never duplicated and often imitated
The replicas aren't real,
There's only one VaKation!

The Moment...

August 28, 2011 at 7:03pm

Seize the moment...
Put an end to the awkward silence
Suspended all actions and activities, etiquettes
If it doesn't concern grinding in the present tense
A breath of fresh air and a dose of erotic medicine,
Forecasting...
Rain and thunderstorms like a weatherman
I'm walking toward your door
The vibration from your legs is telling me
You wanted to let me in,
But you heard I was a VaKation
So for a moment you were hesitant
But you proceed in the present and confirmed your presence
Take cover under covers
NO COVER!!!
I love her, but I don't cuff her
Cuff her when I cut her
Skin tone is golden butter, red bone, or chocolate covered
"The best," is what she uttered.
I accepted without rebuttal...

Inside

March 20, 2014 at 9:56am

I eased inside of her mind & body with a purpose
Flexing her pelvis...
She took it with patience

Pulling and pushing
She loved the pleasure in pain.
Thunderstorms in the forecast
Predicting heavy showers of rain

Her heart thumping... legs shaking...
Her body throbbing in unison...
Her body's calling my name...
Her essence ran down my frame...
As if soaking me was her aim

Dual Penetration

November 19, 2013 at 10:24pm

I want to penetrate your mind & body at the same time
Like love that never leaves
Like sleeping inside of you
While you're wrapped around the idea of me
Inside of your mind and your thighs at the same
I want to be at the center of your core
The encore when you want more
The actions of your thoughts
The process of foreplay three to four times a day
Sharing thoughts and one body for a lifetime

Chemistry

October 2, 2013 at 7:07pm

Creating scenarios
Switching up the scenery
To keep the steam steady
She's completely into me
And I'm equally deep into her
Our desire is to make love mentally with our souls
Causing metamorphic mountains to erupt
Like hot lava within volcanoes
At the core of our situation, temperatures peek
Where metals turn into a liquid state
And we dissolve into steam and breath each other in again

The Definition of Beauty

August 10, 2013 at 7:51pm

My attention was altered and taken captive
By the charisma of the goddess Aphrodite
She completely consumed my thoughts
And rendered me speechless
As she approached me with haste
She placed her finger over my lips
We locked eyes and instantly I could feel her affection
The definition of beauty is all that came to mind
As I entered her heaven and gave her hell

Speechless

Speechless...
Without words she described our escapade
Using only her expressions
Overwhelmed instantaneously by elated memories
Obtained only moments ago

And this is only an intermission
Her intervention...
Will follow shortly after
Now we've arrived at the second chapter
Completely exhausted...
Her new addiction
It's taken such a hold of her subconsciously
That it directly affects what she senses
About me...

She eats and breathes me
Says she needs me
But I keep it calm, cool, and easy
Only supplying her needs

She told me no matter where she is or goes
She would drop everything just to get to where I go
Speechless...

Perfect Sex

Her seductive silhouette demanded my attention, and
Transferred my words into verbs
Switching subjects into predicates
Leaving proper etiquette
Now I think I'm an addict
No Fiction, pragmatic
As word would have it, I need her; tragic
Her touch is like magic
I form fit her insides when she rides, no elastic
I mean I got to have it
While she's here within my reach
I got to grasp it
We started in the bed
Now it's like sweaty sex everywhere
Without a care
Between your thighs, I'm buried there
My fingers in your hair
We're feeling everything, everywhere
Perfect Sex

Life

Yourself: Alone

March 15, 2011 at 7:16pm

Baby, don't be concerned with the concerns and com-
ments of the census...
They're at home by themselves ...
Their opinions shouldn't count...
Their negative nonsense in their context is influencing
your conscience ... Just think for yourself...

The effects of others can affect you...
Self-inflicting wounds keep bleeding...

It hurts me to see you this way
You did it to yourself and only you can fix it... I'm here
for you, but not here for you...
You decided yourself...
Their opinions were senseless...
Now you're at home alone collecting your senses
Counting your cents
Fully aware of the consequences of your actions
Alone

Confident

October 26, 2010 at 9:57pm

Classified as a rare stone...
Her existence is rarely spotted, and her origin is unknown...
She doesn't need me and she doesn't mind being alone...
But the mystery of her independence is what mimics me
mentally and really turns me on....
Clearly she's one of a kind, and I'd be lying to say that I'm
not trying
But really, I'm not trying, I'm pursing you...

Good Morning Beautiful
What's new with you..
How was your day? Did anything special or unusual...
Happen?
Don't spare me any details
Over the phone, through text, or emails

I can even see her subconsciously
With my eyes closed vividly remembering every detail...
Things that make you smile and laugh baby do tell...
What we do in secret I won't tell
Heads or tail we both prevail in ecstasy...
Especially when I'm feeling you and you're feeling me...
Approach & proceed with caution
Her confidence killin' shit!!

Concept

October 8, 2010 at 7:46pm

Erotic thoughts fill my mind like melodies...
I felt her down to the letter...
Be easy calm, cool, collective... At ease...
Fine

Like the summer breeze makes me feel...
The black keys and the white notes make music
And produce intimate and seductive scenes...
I see I'm consumed by her...
Her smiles gives me IN-TER-G(energy)
I breathe her in...
I've lost myself

In her and I can't see My vision is blurred I can't eat...
I awoke in a cold sweat hoping to find her next to me
And the concept of this concept
It was all a dream... I am all alone

Broken

January 4, 2013 at 1:37pm

While passing by, I caught the eye of a stranger, and
could see her spirit had been broken.
Her eyes were swollen, and
She had a hole where her soul used to go.

Torn and ripped open,
She lost her emotions a long time ago.
And as time would go,
She even lost the feeling for living.

She loved her children, but...
Hated the condition she had them in, and...
Who she had them with
But on the night shift she just looked down...

I don't want to be her man
I don't have to be her friend
I just want to make her smile
And laugh for a while
Before she heads back to that...

A Glimpse

November 28, 2012 at 9:39pm

Caught a glimpse of perfection
Now I'm trying to grasp it

Turn her life around and bend her thoughts over backwards
She's confused and need direction like an atlas and
I feel compelled to be MapQuest

Our chemistry matches like matches
We fuel the flames of intimacy
To the fire of destiny with love, faith and trust but
Don't forget about the lust...

Physically, I adorn you
Emotionally I would give my life for you
Because God knows to be faithful and loyal is the fruit of
good soil... And to take it for granted good fruits spoil...

Living a Lie...

September 15, 2012 at 5:43am

Heard about you through the grapevine
Started admiring you for your mind...
You thought it was a line, and that I was lying...
Text, emails, and landlines
My phone is dying, but you're online

I'm getting the vibe that you're living life,
but you're not really alive.

And you're used to lies
I can see the pain in your eyes,
But the smile on your face is so bright
How do you compromise?

I realize telling you about yourself should be a pardon of mine
But to continue letting you live a lie would be wrong of me
And for that...
I apologize.

Silenced...

August 19, 2012 at 2:45pm

Silenced by the sight of her all I see is confidence, and she's not even confident...
A couple of blemishes and scars left her scared
But the story behind them is what made her so interesting
And the fact that your physical shows your character isn't at all diminishing...
She deserves to be happy just because...
Without an agenda with someone outside of her gender that will be genuine and
That isn't a pretender...
She heard a similar story,
But his actions were nowhere near the same
He exceeded the typical,
And open her up to new views and caress her bare essentials...
Mentally and physically capacity
Literally

*??? *

April 7, 2012 at 7:45pm

Without a word spoken I feel your presence
even in this present tense...
Discerning your intentions but trying to make sense of
this mess I'm in...
The mass of men may mask themselves,
but I never blend in with the shadows...
Whether horns or halos,
don't save your "I say so" for me.....
Save your soul for you

Unresponsive to the threats and ridicules
Thank God for the change because if not,
There's no telling the things that would've happen to you
The things men do when they're faced with obstacles of
obsession
And the real lesson is to listen
But their own image affects their vision
Imprisoned by their own thoughts...
To only things they thought
Forgetting what was taught
By making their own laws

RNS...

April 4, 2012 at 2:16pm

Supplies are limited...
And trends change everyday
And their definition of real change
Like the necklace on their neck...
But when it gets hot and tight around their neck
The pressure bust pipes ...because they were basically
Backed up and full of shit and
On the surface they say this is as real as it gets...
But if that's real I don't recognize shit and Stevie ain't
got to wonder he can ask Ray... Because real isn't some-
thing you got to say
Even if you're blinded from birth, you can feel i in your
veins
So don't go by the expressions on their face
RNS

Directions...

February 22, 2012 at 5:03pm

I saw it before I did it
So my direction was God given
And hard times with a peace of mind
Were just a part of living
Started walking in my path
And the math was already mapped out
My mistakes and struggles only brought my best out
I've always been a stand out
Never a stand in for the head count, No-handouts
Any stress I experience, I bottled it up and pour it out
So my words hold reverence
And you can understand from what aspect I speak about

Highs and Lows

October 26, 2011 at 11:18am

Sometimes the weight of this world
Has me feenin' for my last breathe
Forgive me for all my sins and my past lefts
Lord Knows I am running a race
Nonstop... never hesitant through these street lights
Street life keeps calling my name,
but because of these kids I think twice
Will they remember me or martyr my ideology
Obviously some shit to which you fake niggas can't relate
I understand your hate and debate
Your ways to change your life
The roll of dice is only by chance
I'm trying to escape that life
See I'm on some high through the low type shit
You throw bricks and expect shit
You wouldn't do for yourself
If the shoes were switched it couldn't fit
But before I let these niggas pull me down...
I'll close my eyes and put me down

The Dream

October 6, 2011 at 11:45pm

With dreams that reach the sky,
I set standards to a new horizon
Looking beyond the faded figures of the clouds...
Into open fields of opportunity where the
Possibilities of a positive end are endless
As I strive for perfection within my reflection
I see what it could be, or what it will be
Never stopping to be detracted on what it is
Because what it is
Is a lot of struggling, hardships, and hard times...
That's why I position my mind
To a better place at a different time.

The Things

September 16, 2011 at 1:57am

The things men do to please the ones for which they lust
Are the same things women do when they're willing and
ready to fuck
Luring behind white lies
Love, tell me I'm lying
After a few failed attempts, what's the use in you trying?
It's all a game and you've seen it all before...
Nothing new to you
Meanwhile, on one side you're confident,
And on the other hand you're insecure
Lower your guard let me in to get through to you
I would never build you up to break you down,
or make you submissive...
I'm not that individual
I think you're beautiful
From your roots down to your cuticles
If only you could see the view I have of you
Through my eyes you would love it too
I could tell you all the things I would do to you, but
You would call those just words
Adverbs and reiterate actions of those thoughts.
Deliberately, gently, deeply and repeatedly
Giving the assurance that this chemistry
Is a result of intimacy
When love calls...

How Do You?

July 15, 2014 at 11:03am

"How do you?"
I'm intrigued by how your mind works,
And how your emotions paint pictures.
So vivid, that a blind man could create the masterpiece on
canvas...

How can your heart withhold so much pressure,
And not collapse; remaining functional?
How do you show so much love through it,
Though I can clearly see it's broken?

How do you...
Deal with the pain and still smile at the same time?
How do you...
Take in the pleasure and contain the rain at the same time?
How do you?

Placement

June 3, 2014 at 7:22am

Heaven knows my soul has endured a load that was not my own...

Far from home, and alone

I've longed for love and almost loss my goals...

I've loaned out all my gold

Looking for life in all the wrong places, circles and spaces

I need placement, or

Just a place to find peace

Puzzled

October 27, 2013 at 5:35pm

If you took the time to look into her eyes
Even behind the smile

You would see the hurt and the pain
The real reason why she cries,
Wipes her eyes, and tells everyone she's alright...
She lies
...but since some people can't but trusted
She's quiet...
So the hurt and pain compiles inside
Into concrete walls of lies and materialistic insignificance
She sighs...
Her struggle is that her strength was that
She was able to hold up a facade for so long, and
He could understand her language because he dreamed
About her and this situation
Before he ever saw her face...

Justified Dreams

September 5, 2013 at 11:59am

I justified my actions by the means of C.R.E.A.M
I had a dream that I saw death watching me
In the form of my being
I was on the block off 16th, it was 6:15, and
My auntie asked me if I wanted something eat…
I turn my back toward the street, and
A black Cadillac with black tinted windows
Rolled down the window
I saw a black hoodie and my own face
Peeked out the window
Yelling "I am my brother's keeper…" as I empty the clip.
My breath began getting shorter
I could hear my own heartbeat…
I start choking on what tasted like my own blood…
My body felt cold
My lips felt numb and my vision got blurry
Mental pictures filled my memory
As faded images surrounded me
I screamed!
I could hear my nieces, nephews, godson and daughter
All calling my name in unison,
But I couldn't keep my eyes opened…
I woke up in a cold sweat,
And drove off in my black Cadillac and black hoodie…

Justice

July 16, 2013 at 3:07pm

We're all praying for justice
I'm praying we aren't prey
I represent for Trayvon Martin,
And all the others like us dying without a face.
Thousands of young African Americans died last year
to gun violence, Most without a case,
But you never heard their names.
Parents still crying, their children can't be replaced
When we pray and ask God for guidance, do we really
believe in change?
Or are we justifying the means of our actions until we
become the ones slain? I'm not perfect by any means,
but I mean what I say
We all need God, but we can't agree on HIS name
What I do know is
Being absent from the body and present with the Lord
is gain

West Side

May 30, 2013 at 12:06pm

A young man and his lady
were strapped with their baby across his chest
Walking under the street lights
On the West.....

Niggas strapped with techs
Equipped with clips and vest
See... You see Life and Death
More or less walking down the West...

Different sets
B'z and GDz
Good green and crystal meth
Hoes selling they souls
And aren't even in high school yet
Niggas cut your throat
And swear they're your folks
Get smoked by your own bro on this side...

Popping pills, sippin' liquor pouring wine
Celebrating life
Living to die...
Some sniffing them lines
Living a lie,
We're living in prime, not prey
We pray
On the West Side

Can You Help Me?

May 23, 2013 at 1:00pm

I saw death in the form of a white woman
Walking down the West
I wondered why she shook her head,
And talked to herself
She said she hadn't fucked with that white Girl
Since she was a young white girl and
She'd smoked her first man
When she was just about grown
Now she's addicted to that glass dick
Wondering where it's at
She said he raped her mind and kissed her soul
Now she can't stop playing with death

As she cries with a loud voice she says,
"He loves me and he makes me feel like a little girl.
I'm special to him and no one else.
Nothing seems to matter to me but him.
I can't control it.
Can you help me?"

Hanging In the Balance

May 10, 2013 at 4:30am

Walking in these shadows of darkness
I can't see anything!
It's like my eyes are closed, covered, and shut
Completely dysfunctional
So I hold on to my faith and my pistol
Seeing that I'm a pistol packing believer, and
I believe that these shells
Hold enough heat to make you think about hell
I got my sword tatted on my chest
Psalms 51:10-15
All five verses
"Protected by Heaven"
On my wrist…
"Only God Can Judge Me"
On my neck...
I got my head up, a clip in my car door,
One in my sock and don't even need it
Lord forgive me if I'm mistaken and misunderstood
I don't know the time, and People don't know their place
I don't have the patience to show
My shortcomings are longer than the rivers run deep
Hide my hunger and understand my need
I'm paralyzed by these perilous times
Guide me according to the FAITH and not my faith!
Selah

Religion

May 9, 2013 at 11:07am

In the silence of the night
All he could hear was her crying
It drove him crazy and left him confused
Because he was her child, and her concern

Her prayers, hopes, and wishes
Weren't enough to put her in position
She needed a relationship with God
But all she knew was a religion

To Whom It May Concern

Truth is, most of the time you're on my mind and
Although most times you can't reply,
I do read between lines
Your pretty brown eyes, amazing smile and that
Style that's so close to mine
I'd be lying if I said I wasn't trying to keep you around
But the real question is, "Baby, how can I be down?"

I Luv U

In theory we're already closer than most,
But closer than close isn't close enough
See you knew me before all the similes, metaphors,
phrases and quotes
Even the words I've spoken
Were only able to briefly describe you
No details...
That's why I compose these words like emails
Inhale, then exhale, and send them off...
Any pains or stress I felt you knock it off...
I would love to keep you all to myself,
But I realize you are so much bigger than me
You're heaven sent,
So my jealously concerning you is irreverent
But somehow conflicts with my common sense
Yet, the only way I can release this bitterness
Is to tell you and to let you know
I luv u...
I luv u poetry!

The End

Hold fast to dreams,

For if dreams die

Life is a broken-winged bird,

That cannot fly…

-Langston Hughes

BIBLIOGRAPHY

Ron Whitaker Jr., the youngest of 6 siblings from a small North East town in Texas, was instilled with the moral values of God, family, love, and loyalty. Being the youngest of 6 siblings, he was always known for being a watcher, a good listener, and a mediator.

Coming from small town (DeKalb ,TX) and a humble beginning, life had its ups and downs and as individuals we all deal with our situations the best of our knowledge and ability . One day Mr. Whitaker attended a poem night at Skyward Lounge in Texarkana, Arkansas, where he listened to several artists performing their own spoken word poetry. While snapping his fingers he was confronted by a man named "Tank." Tank told Mr. Whitaker, "I bet you could do that…" not knowing that it was something he always wanted to do but he was nervous.

Ron eventually performed and took on the stage name, *VaKation,* representing his ability to captivate his audience through his words and voice to create a vivid picture; often causing those listening to go on a mental vacation. From the seed planted that night by "Tank," his dream, this book, came to fruition.

Thank you for your purchase of this book.

For more information on Ron Whitaker, Jr. aka VaKation or to
order autographed copies of this book, visit

www.CollegeBoyPublishing.com

To order other titles visit

www.CollegeBoyPublishing.com

COLLEGE BOY
PUBLISHING

"We Breed Bestsellers"

www.ingramcontent.com/pod-product-compliance
Lightning Source LLC
LaVergne TN
LVHW051813080426
835513LV00017B/1932